Just Mom and Me

The tear-out, punch-out, fill-out book of fun for girls and their moms

★ American Girl®

Published by American Girl Publishing, Inc.
Copyright © 2008 by American Girl, LLC

Questions or comments? Call 1-800-845-0005, visit our Web site at americangirl.com,
or write to Customer Service, American Girl, 8400 Fairway Place, Middleton, WI 53562-0497.

Printed in China
08 09 10 11 12 13 LEO 10 9 8 7 6 5 4 3

Editorial Development: Erin Falligant
Art Direction & Design: Chris Lorette David
Production: Mindy Rappe, Gretchen Krause, Kendra Schluter, Jeannette Bailey, Judith Lary
Illustrations: Stacy Peterson

Special thanks to Patti Kelley Criswell

Dear Reader,

This book's for you and the girl who knows you best—your mom. Whether you have five minutes in the car or a weekend to spend together, make the most of your time with these quizzes, games, and fun ideas. You'll even find notes and gift coupons to tear out and share with each other.

Ready for some girl time? Make a Mom-and-me date and then make it great!

Your friends at American Girl

This or That

Check off the things you like best, and ask your mom to do the same. How many answers do you have in common?

**Tear out and fill out the following lists—
one for you and one for your mom!**

Dinner Out

Get all dressed up, even if you're going to a pizza joint. Vow that you'll each try a bite of something you've never tried before. After dinner, be restaurant critics. Take turns describing the restaurant and rating it, from four stars for a great dining experience to one star for a not-so-fine time.

Movie Night

Watching movies at home? Turn down the lights, turn off the cell phone, and dress up a batch of freshly popped corn with one of the toppers on the next page. It will taste so good, you'll think you're at the theater!

Tear out these cards so that you're ready for your next movie night with Mom.

Stovetop Popcorn

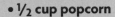

You will need:
- an adult to help you
- large pot with tight-fitting lid
- oven mitts
- ½ cup popcorn
- 3 tablespoons cooking oil

Pour oil and 1 to 2 kernels of popcorn into pot with lid, and heat on high. When the kernels pop, pour remaining popcorn into pan and replace lid. When popcorn begins popping, slip on oven mitts and have an adult help you shake pan. Place one hand on lid and and lift pot with other hand. Shake pan a few times, return it to heat for 30 seconds, and shake pan again. As soon as popcorn stops popping, remove pan from heat.

Popcorn Toppers

You will need:
- an adult to help you
- 6 cups stovetop or microwave popcorn in a paper bag
- your choice of toppings:

Cinnamon Twist—¼ cup sugar, ½ teaspoon cinnamon
Easy Cheese—2 tablespoons powdered cheese topping
Tex Mix—1 teaspoon taco seasoning, 2 tablespoons powdered cheese topping

Have an adult add topping to the bag, seal, and shake.

Movies We Want to See

Write down the movies you want to watch with Mom, and keep this list in your purse or hers.

Now We're Cookin'!

Imagine that you're on a cooking show. As you make dinner with Mom, describe to your audience what you're doing.

Trading Places

Interview your mom about the kind of girl she was. Then trade places with her and imagine yourself as a grown-up.

Tear out the following checklists, and interview each other to fill in the blanks.

When You Were My Age
(ask your mom)

- What you spent your allowance on

- Stuffed animal or doll
  you couldn't sleep without

- Pet you had or dreamed of having

- Best friends

- Food your parents made you eat

- Best school subject

- Worst school subject

- Least-favorite chore

- Funkiest fashion you followed

- Most embarrassing moment

When You Are My Age
(ask your daughter)

• Where you will live
_____

• Job you hope to have
_____

• House rule you'll make
_____

_____

• House rule you'll break
_____

_____

• Pets you will have
_____

• Number of children you'd like to have
_____

• What you would name a daughter
_____

• Advice you'd give her
_____

_____

_____

• Allowance you'd pay her
_____

• How you'd make her earn it
_____

Seesaw Stories

Read one of these story starters out loud. Take turns adding sentences to the story until one of you declares "the end."

(Your name here) ripped through the wrapping paper and squealed with delight. "Oh, Mom!" she cried. "I've always wanted a . . ."

(Your name here) stared at the pile of broken glass and took a deep breath. "O.K., Mom," she said. "Here's what really happened."

It looked like ordinary meat loaf, but it was actually Mom's top-secret recipe. One bite would give (your name here) the ability to . . .

When (your name here) and her mother signed up for the reality TV show, they never thought they'd have to . . .

(Your name here) shivered as she followed her mother down the dark, narrow staircase. The air felt cold, almost as if . . .

Then
&
Now

How did your mom look when she was your age? Find a photo of her as a girl, and compare it to a photo of you now.

Tape a photo behind each window, and then slide this page into a 5 x 7 picture frame.

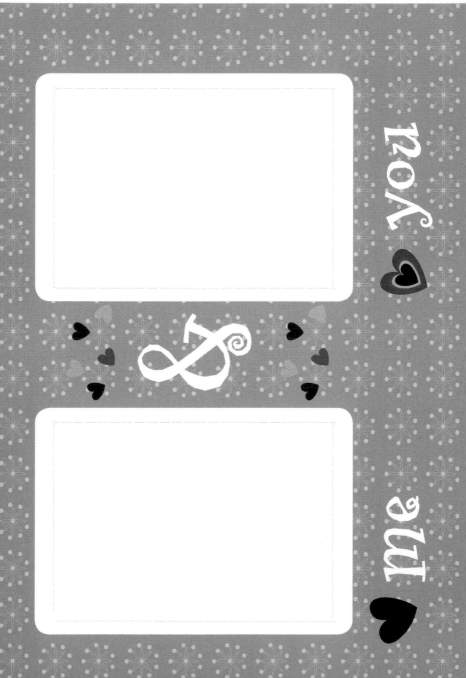

Shop
& Save

Go shopping at a garage sale
or secondhand store, and try
to create outfits for under $10
each. When you get home, look
through ads and catalogues to
figure out how much money
you might have spent on
the outfits brand-new.
Surprised?

Recipe for Fun

Search through cookbooks and choose a new recipe to try. Or ask your mom to teach you how to make one of Grandma's tried-and-true dishes. Head to the grocery store to find ingredients, and whip them up in the kitchen together.

Create new recipes or write down your favorites on the tear-out recipe cards.

a "Mom & Me"
recipe for:

a "Mom & Me"
recipe for:

a "Mom & Me"
recipe for:

Puzzle
Marathon

Tackle a puzzle with lots
of pieces. Find a place to set
it up and leave it out until it's
done. How quickly can you
finish it together?

Don't Peek!

Sit with your back to your mom, and answer questions about what she looks like today. Ask her to do the same for you. Then take a good look at each other. How'd you do?

Tear out the following checklists, and fill them out at the same time.

My mom

- Is she wearing something in her hair?
  ❑ yes   ❑ no

- Does she have glasses on? ❑ yes   ❑ no

- Is she wearing earrings? ❑ yes   ❑ no

- Is she wearing ❑ a dress   ❑ a skirt
                  ❑ pants   ❑ shorts

- What color is her shirt or dress?

  _____

- What kind of shoes is she wearing?

  _____

- Is she wearing socks? ❑ yes   ❑ no

- Is she wearing a necklace? ❑ yes   ❑ no

- Is she wearing a bracelet? ❑ yes   ❑ no

- If so, which wrist is it on? ❑ left   ❑ right

My daughter

- Is she wearing something in her hair?
  ❑ yes   ❑ no

- Does she have glasses on? ❑ yes   ❑ no

- Is she wearing earrings? ❑ yes   ❑ no

- Is she wearing ❑ a dress   ❑ a skirt
                  ❑ pants   ❑ shorts

- What color is her shirt or dress?

  _____

- What kind of shoes is she wearing?

  _____

- Is she wearing socks? ❑ yes   ❑ no

- Is she wearing a necklace? ❑ yes   ❑ no

- Is she wearing a bracelet? ❑ yes   ❑ no

- If so, which wrist is it on? ❑ left   ❑ right

License to Laugh

The next time you're in the car, come up with silly phrases to match the letters of the license plates you see. "BAE" might mean "beans and eggs." "PDM" might mean "polka-dotted monkey." Your turn!

Sweet
Surprises

Tuck one of these little notes into your mom's briefcase or coat pocket. Fold it, sign it, and seal it with a kiss.

hi

hola ✽ ahoj
salut ✽ ciao
hallo ✽ aloha
konnichiwa
hej ✽ hei

Someone's
thinking about
you today.

ME!

S.W.A.K.
(Sealed with a Kiss)

Mom & Me

To________________________

From____________________

S.W.A.K.
(Sealed with a Kiss)

Mom & Me

To________________________

From____________________

Take note:

I love you!

Tag— you're it!

Pass this back to me in a super-secret way.

S.W.A.K.
(Sealed with a Kiss)

Mom & Me

To________________________

From_____________________

S.W.A.K.
(Sealed with a Kiss)

Mom & Me

To________________________

From_____________________

This note is

a hug

from me to you.
Can you feel it?

Hope your day is full of

sweet
surprises!

Mom & Me

To_____

From_____

S.W.A.K. (sealed with a kiss)

Mom & Me

To_____

From_____

Smile!

Somebody loves you.

(Guess who?)

UR $\dfrac{\begin{array}{c} 2 \text{ sweet} \\ 2 \text{ be} \end{array}}{4 \text{ gotten}}$

Pop
Quiz

Pull out one of your graded tests or worksheets, and quiz your mom to see if she can answer the questions. How'd she do? Did she learn anything new?

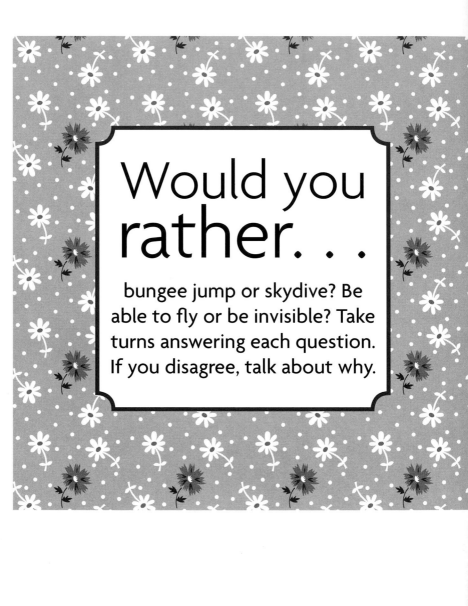

Would you rather. . .

bungee jump or skydive? Be able to fly or be invisible? Take turns answering each question. If you disagree, talk about why.

Would you rather . . .

. . . go backward in time or forward in time?

. . . dance in front of 10,000 people or sing in front of them?

. . . eat all meals at home or all meals at restaurants?

. . . be able to talk to animals or have any animal you wanted as a pet?

. . . be an only child or have ten siblings?

. . . be president of the United States or the queen of England?

. . . be able to see the future or be able to read people's minds?

. . . live in a tree house or live on a boat?

Our Family Tree

How much do you know about your roots? Ask your mom to help you write the names of your family members on these leaves. (Make a color copy of the leaves **before** you write on them if you think you'll need more.) Punch out the leaves, and hang them from a paper tree on a bulletin board or the back of your bedroom door.

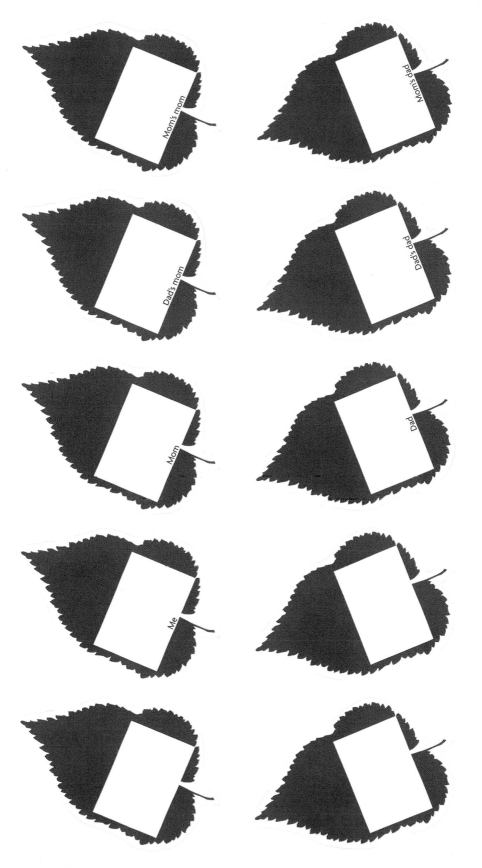

Turn
Old into
New

Go shopping in your own
closets. Look through
magazines to check out
new styles, and then try to
create them with clothes
you already own.
Snap photos of your
silliest and most
stylish outfits.

Family
Favorites

Can you guess your
mom's favorite things?
Can she guess yours?
And how much do you
have in common?

Tear out the lists, and give the
second one to your mom
to fill out.

Me

	Mine	Mom's
• Favorite pizza topping		
• Favorite sport		
• Favorite sandwich		
• Favorite TV show		
• Favorite holiday		
• Favorite vegetable		
• Favorite song		
• Favorite color		
• Favorite candy		
• Favorite animal		
• Favorite movie star		

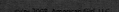

Mom

	Mine	My daughter's
• Favorite pizza topping		
• Favorite sport		
• Favorite sandwich		
• Favorite TV show		
• Favorite holiday		
• Favorite vegetable		
• Favorite song		
• Favorite color		
• Favorite candy		
• Favorite animal		
• Favorite movie star		

Mom's the Word

Play tic-tac-toe, but instead of X's, use M's. Try to win by getting three of your letters in a row OR by spelling the word "MOM."

At-Home
Spa

Put on your robes and pull back your hair. Play soothing music. Then whip up these homemade concoctions, and settle in for a stress-free afternoon with Mom.

Tear out the recipe cards so that you'll be ready for your next at-home spa day.

Banana Mash Mask
for your face

You will need:
- **1 ½ ripe bananas**
- **2 teaspoons honey**

Mash the bananas in a bowl with a fork. (Don't overmash, or the mask will be too runny.) Mix in the honey. Spread the mask on your face and let it sit for 10 minutes or until dry. Rinse clean with lukewarm water, and gently apply a bit of moisturizing lotion.

Sugar Scrub
for your hands

You will need:
- **3 tablespoons sugar**
- **2 tablespoons baby oil**

Mix sugar and oil to make a paste. Wet your hands, and scoop some of the paste into the palm of one hand. Rub the mixture between your palms and on the backs of your hands and fingers. Rinse with warm water and pat dry.

Lemon Soak
for your hands

You will need:
- **an adult to help you**
- **1 cup milk**
- **1 tablespoon lemon juice**

Ask an adult to heat the milk on the stove or in a microwave just until warm. Pour lemon juice and warm milk into a small bowl. Soak fingertips in the bowl for 5 to 10 minutes. Rinse off with warm water and pat dry. Rub lotion onto your hands and nails.

A Year of You & Me

Make a calendar featuring your twelve favorite photos of you and your mom. Look for design-your-own calendars at craft stores, or print off blank calendar pages from the Internet. You can also take your photos to a photo lab to have your calendar printed.

Making
Music

Ask someone (other than your mom) to help you burn a CD of songs that both you and your mom like. Every year for your mom's birthday, create a new CD to add to her music collection.

Tear out one of these covers, fill in the playlist on the back, and slide the cover into the front of a CD case.

Music We Agree On

To: _____

From: _____

Date: _____

Music We Agree On

To: _____

From: _____

Date: _____

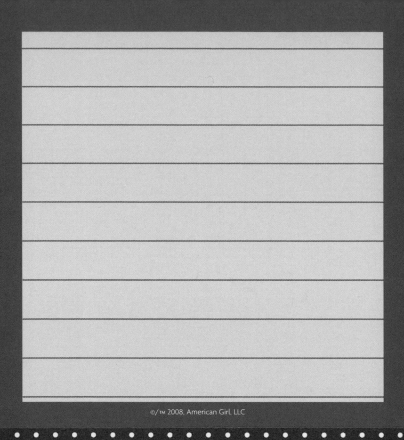

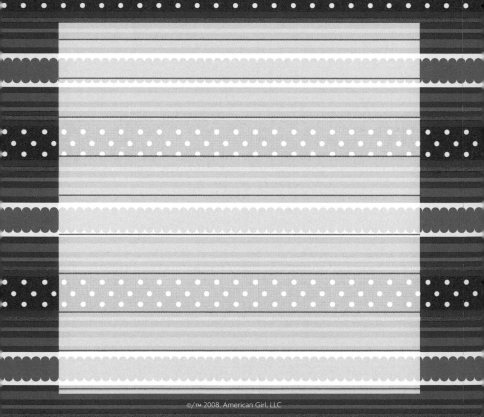

Feel-Good
Box

Plan ahead for days when you or your mom is feeling blue. Decorate a shoe box, and work together to fill it with things that make you smile. Add a photo of the two of you, a comic strip, and sweet surprises, such as bubble gum or lollipops. Keep adding to the box so that whenever one of you needs it, there's something new inside.

Feel-Good
Box

Tear-&-Share Coupons

Give your mom the gift of special time with you. Tear out one of these coupons, and tuck it into a card for her. Ask her to recycle the coupons by giving them back to you someday.

Have a Hug

This coupon is good for one big bear hug.

Funny Face

This coupon is good for a silly face
to make you smile.

Neck Rub

This coupon is good for a 15-minute massage.

Remember When

Pull out an old photo album, and take turns telling stories about when you were younger. Spot something in a photo that you used to love to do with Mom? Try it again today, just for fun. Build a fort, finger paint, or have a tea party.

Peace, Please

Share these door hangers so that you and your mom can ask for alone time when you need it.

Tear out one of the door hangers. Punch out the perforated circle before sliding the hanger onto a doorknob.

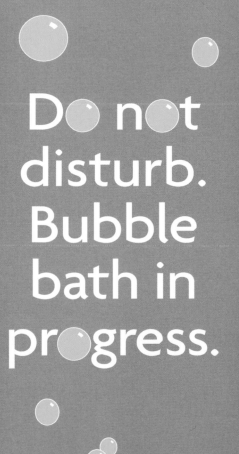

Do not disturb. Bubble bath in progress.

Shhh! I'm resting or thinking or sleeping or daydreaming.

(Thanks!)

Take a Virtual Trip

You don't have to leave home to feel as if you did. Pick a country on a globe or map, and research it online with your mom. Make recipes and try a few traditions from the area. If the language spoken there is different from your own, learn a new word or two.

Book Buddies

Read books together in bed or in another cozy place. Take turns reading aloud from the same book. Or read your own books and stop to share silly or exciting parts with each other.

Tear out the purple bookmark, and fill it with words that your mom will want to read again and again. Have her fill out the pink one for you!

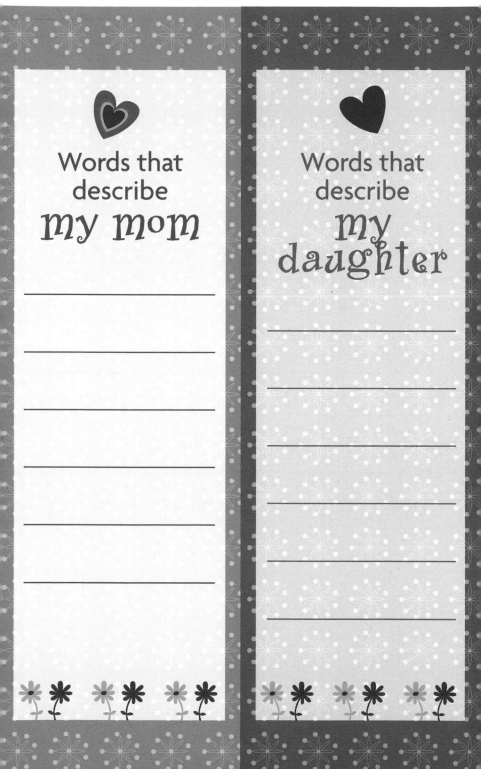

Words that describe
my mom

Words that describe
my daughter

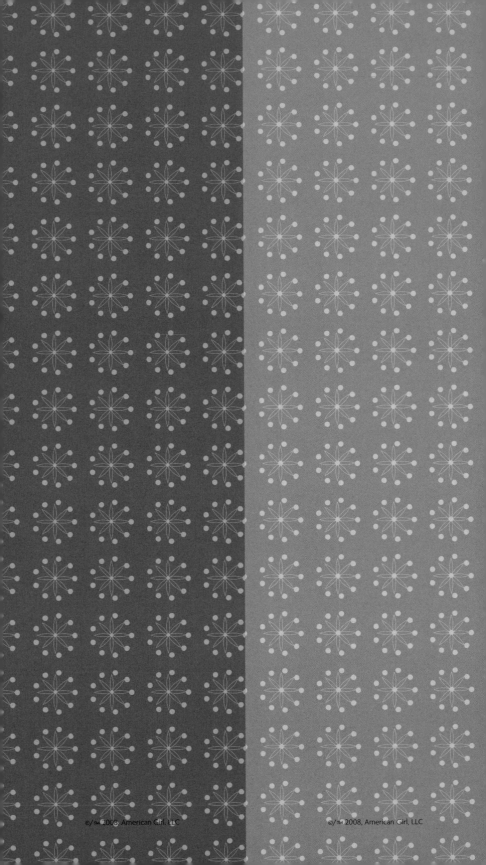

Seesaw Stories

Read one of these story starters out loud. Take turns adding sentences to the story until one of you declares "the end."

"It's for you!" Mom called up the stairs. When (your name here) picked up the phone, she couldn't believe her ears. It was . . .

So many strange things had been happening around the house lately. (Your name here) was beginning to suspect that her mother was . . .

When Mom turned her back, Jasper lifted his paw and winked at (your name here). He seemed to be saying . . .

(Your name here) tried to close the lid of her over-stuffed suitcase. "It's cold on the planet Earth," said her mother. "Don't forget to pack your . . ."

(Your name here) let go of her mother's hand and stepped through the doorway. The first thing she saw was . . .

Jar of Fun

When you think of something you'd like to do with your mom, write it on a slip of paper. Ask her to do the same. Toss your ideas into a clean, empty jar. When you have time together, pull out an idea and give it a try!

Start your jar with the ideas on the next page, and then add some of your own.

start a collection	teach each other a dance
talk about the day you were born	make up new names for each other for a day
start a new holiday tradition	make up a silly song
play hopscotch	jump rope
make up a family cheer	do each other's hair
go to a girls' or women's sporting event	give each other shoulder massages
look at the clouds and describe what you see	try to make each other laugh
take 5 deep breaths	bake something to share with neighbors
do yoga or Pilates	blow bubbles

Jar of Fun

Jar of Fun

Jar of Fun

Jar of Fun

Jar of Fun

Jar of Fun

Jar of Fun

Jar of Fun

Jar of Fun

Jar of Fun

Jar of Fun

Jar of Fun

Jar of Fun

Jar of Fun

Jar of Fun

Jar of Fun

When You're Both Busy

Create something together that you can each add to on your own. Leave one of these works-in-progress where you both can see it, such as on the kitchen counter or on the refrigerator door.

- Write a story together, taking turns adding sentences.

- Complete a color-by-number poster, each of you using different-colored crayons or markers.

- Work on a word search or crossword puzzle, taking turns circling or filling in words.

- Doodle or write messages to each other on a write-on, wipe-off board.

- Fill out a journal together. Write about your day, and then leave space for Mom to write about hers. It's the next best thing to spending the day together.

Order Up!

Pretend that you work at a restaurant. Decide what tonight's specials are, and take your mom's food order. Tie on an apron, and serve her with a smile!

Write down your mom's order on one of these tear-out guest checks.

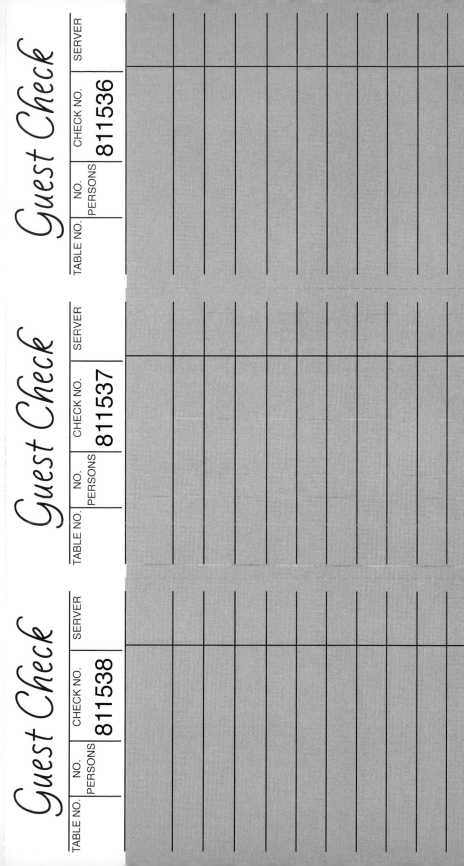

Thank you!
Come again!

Thank you!
Come again!

Thank you!
Come again!

Remember
Today

Make a time capsule that includes
a photo of the two of you
today, a newspaper clipping
from today's paper, and a note
about what you did, ate, and
laughed about. Add two secret
wishes. Seal everything in a safe
place and then decide when
you'll open it. Will it be a year
from now? Five years?

Add More Green

Where will your garden grow? In your backyard? In a pot on your porch? On your windowsill? Talk with your mom about how much space you have, and decide what you'd like to grow. Shop together for seeds or small plants, and spend the weekend potting and watering them. Then watch and wait!

Slide these signs onto wooden craft sticks and press them into the soil next to the things you've planted.

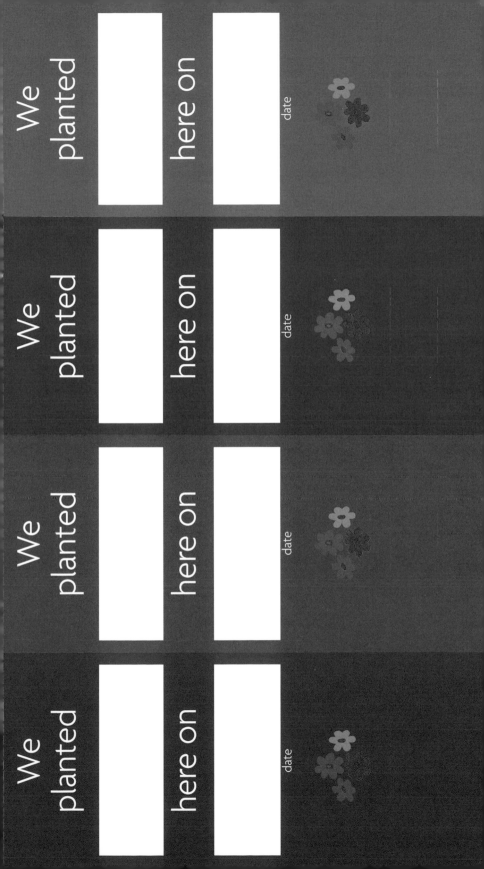

We
planted

here on

date

We
planted

here on

date

We
planted

here on

date

We
planted

here on

date

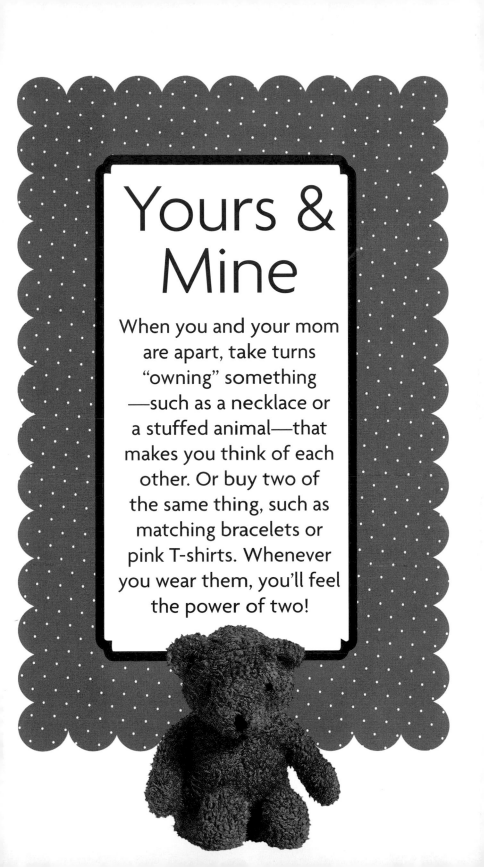

Yours & Mine

When you and your mom are apart, take turns "owning" something —such as a necklace or a stuffed animal—that makes you think of each other. Or buy two of the same thing, such as matching bracelets or pink T-shirts. Whenever you wear them, you'll feel the power of two!

Improve a Room

Decide with your mom how much you have to spend, and then shop at resale or discount shops to find funky furnishings and wall hangings. Or pull out your craft supplies and get creative. Can you wrap new fabric around an old pillow or repaint a picture frame?

Secret Signs

Come up with a signal that only the two of you will understand. Blinking three times might mean "I love you." Two tugs on your ear might mean "pass the ketchup." What other silly signs can you think of?

Make a Pact

This book is ending, but your good times with Mom will go on and on. Sign this pact and post it on the fridge to remind yourselves to stay connected and to make time for fun!

Our Pact

We vow to:

- make the most of our time together,
- set up one-on-one dates every month, and
- laugh together every day.

Signed:

_____
(me)

and

_____
(my mom)

Date: _____

Which mom-and-me quizzes, games, and activities did you like best? What are your favorite things to do with your mom?

Write to us!

Just Mom & Me Editor
American Girl
8400 Fairway Place
Middleton, WI 53562

(All comments and suggestions received by American Girl may be used without compensation or acknowledgment. Sorry—photos can't be returned.)

Here are some other American Girl books you might like:

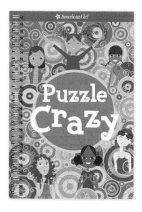

❏ I read it.

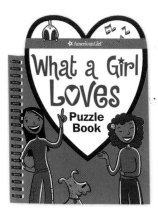

❏ I read it.

❏ I read it.

❏ I read it.

❏ I read it.

❏ I read it.